The Life and Work of...

Paul Klee

Sean Connolly

Heinemann LIBRARY

First published in Great Britain by
Heinemann Library,
Halley Court, Jordan Hill, Oxford OX2 8EJ
a division of Reed Educational and Professional
Publishing Ltd.
Heinemann is a registered trademark of Reed
Educational & Professional Publishing Ltd.

OXFORD MELBOURNE AUCKLAND
JOHANNESBURG BLANTYRE GABORONE
IBADAN PORTSMOUTH (NH) USA CHICAGO

Designed by Celia Floyd
Illustrations by Kim Harley
Printed in Hong Kong/China

03 02 01 00
10 9 8 7 6 5 4 3 2

ISBN 0 431 09176 5

British Library Cataloguing in Publication Data

Connolly, Sean
    Life and work of Paul Klee
    1. Klee, Paul, 1879-1940 – Juvenile literature
    2. Painters – Switzerland – Biography – Juvenile
    literature
    3. Painting, Modern – 20th Century – Switzerland –
    Juvenile literature
    4. Painting, Swiss – Juvenile literature
    I. Title
    759.9'494

For more information about Heinemann Library
books, or to order, please telephone
+44(0)1865 888066, or send a fax to +441865 314091.
You can visit our web site at www.heinemann.co.uk

Acknowledgements
The Publishers would like to thank the following for
permission to reproduce photographs:

AKG Photo, pp. 4, 10, 22, 24
Paul-Klee-Stiftung, Kunstmuseum, Bern/L Moillet,
p.20. Fotopress/Walter Henggeler, p. 28;

Page 5, Paul Klee 'Familienspaziergang, 1930, 264',
Credit: Paul-Klee-Stiftung, Kunstmuseum, Bern.
Page 7, Paul Klee 'Dünen landschaft, 19213, 139',
Credit: Paul-Klee-Stiftung, Kunstmuseum, Bern.
Page 9, Paul Klee 'Schadau, 1895/96', Credit: Paul-
Klee-Stiftung, Kunstmuseum, Bern. Page 11, Paul
Klee 'Siebzehn, irr. 1923', Credit: Oeffentliche
Kunstsammlung Kupferstichkabinett, Basel. Page
13, Paul Klee 'Meine Bude, 1896', Credit: Paul-Klee-
Stiftung, Kunstmuseum, Bern. Page 15, Paul Klee
'Lily, 1905, 32', Credit: Paul-Klee-Stiftung,
Kunstmuseum, Bern. Page 17, Paul Klee, 'Candide
7. Capitel "Il lève le voile d'une main timide" 1911,
63', Credit: Paul-Klee-Stiftung, Kunstmuseum, Bern.
Page 19, Paul Klee 'Mädchen mit Krügen, 1910,
120', Credit: Paul-Klee-Stiftung, Kunstmuseum,
Bern. Page 21, Paul Klee 'Rote und Weisse Kuppeln,
1914, 45', Credit: AKG Photo. Page 23, Paul Klee
'Einst dem Grau der Nacht enttaucht..., 1918, 17',
Credit: Paul-Klee-Stiftung, Kunstmuseum, Bern.
Page 25, Paul Klee 'Plan einer garten-architektur,
1920, 214', Credit: Bridgeman Art Library. Page 27,
Paul Klee 'Polyphon gefasstes Weiss, 1930,
140(x10)', Credit: Paul-Klee-Stiftung, Kunstmuseum,
Bern. Page 29, Paul Klee 'TOD und FEUER, 1940,
332 (G 12), Credit: Paul-Klee-Stiftung,
Kunstmuseum, Bern.

Cover photograph reproduced with permission of
Bridgeman Art Library

Our thanks to Paul Flux for his comments in the
preparation of this book.

Any words appearing in the text in bold, **like this**,
are explained in the Glossary.

Contents

Who was Paul Klee?

Paul Klee was a Swiss painter and **graphic artist**. He liked to make very colourful paintings. These pictures make people think of music and dreams.

Paul kept a sense of fun in his paintings. This picture shows how he liked to 'take a line for a walk'.

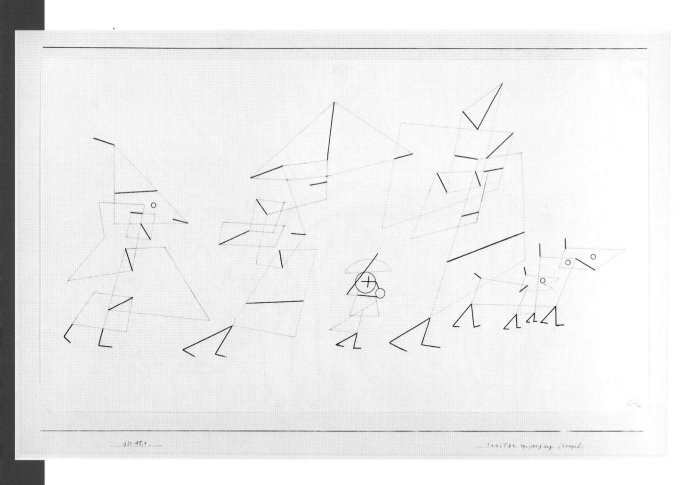

Early years

Paul Klee was born on 18 December 1879 near the city of Berne in Switzerland. His family loved music. Paul learned to play the violin when he was seven years old.

Paul's uncle Ernst had a café. Paul liked to look at the patterns on the tablecloths there. This painting made in 1923 shows Paul was still interested in patterns.

1923 139 Dünen landschaft

School-days

Paul went to school in Berne. He still enjoyed music. He joined the Berne **orchestra** when he was only 10 years old.

Paul also began to like drawing pictures. He filled his school notebooks with drawings and designs. He tried to show his love of music and poetry in his paintings.

The move to Germany

Paul left school when he was 19. He moved to Munich, Germany. There he began to **study** drawing and painting. Magazines like this helped him to think of funny ideas.

Paul had a good sense of humour. This picture was made in 1923 when he was 44 years old. It shows his sense of humour in his work.

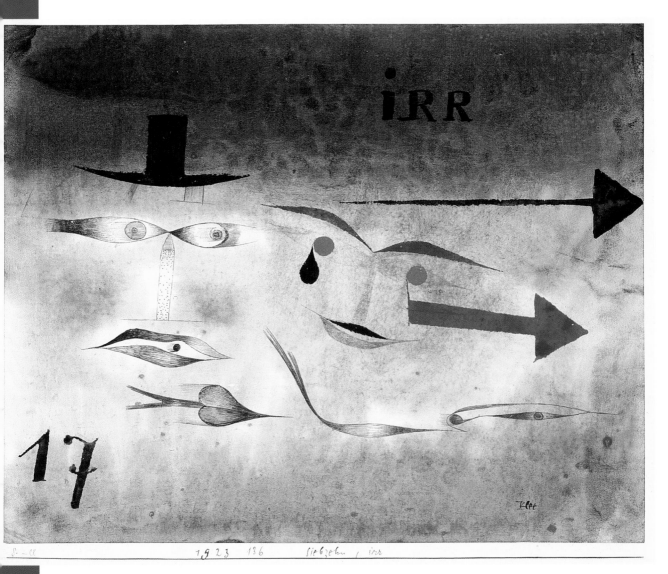

Learning to paint

Paul **studied** paintings in Italy when he was 22 years old. He then returned to his family in Berne. There he **practised** his own art and tried out many different ideas.

Most of Paul's works were drawings or **etchings**.
This drawing of his bedroom shows how well Paul
could draw.

A growing family

In 1906 Paul married Lily Stumpf. Their son Felix was born a year later. Lily earned money by playing piano **concerts**. Paul worked at home.

Some of Paul's **etchings** were **exhibited** in Munich in 1906. Paul became better known after the exhibition. This is a painting of Lily.

Public success

Paul's first one-man **exhibition** was in Berne in 1910. It was a great success. The same exhibition was then shown in other Swiss cities.

Paul's pictures were black and white. He used an ink pen and drew on white paper. This picture was used in a book.

A friendly welcome

Paul became friends with two other artists, August Macke and Wassily Kandinsky. In 1911 Paul joined their group of **expressionist** artists, called Der Blaue Reiter (The Blue Rider).

Paul also liked the work of other artists. He painted this picture in 1910. It looks like a painting by an artist called Paul Cézanne.

Colour takes hold

In 1914 Paul and August Macke visited Tunisia in Africa. Paul loved the bright light and colours there. He decided to stop using just black and white in his pictures.

20

Rote u. weisse Kuppeln 1914.45

This painting shows how Paul began to use colours. The coloured squares look like the **mosaics** he saw in Tunisia.

New directions

Paul was happy painting in many colours. He felt free to try other new ideas too. He started putting letters and numbers in his pictures.

Paul thought numbers and letters made people think of words and dreams. Paul felt he was making a new **language** in his pictures.

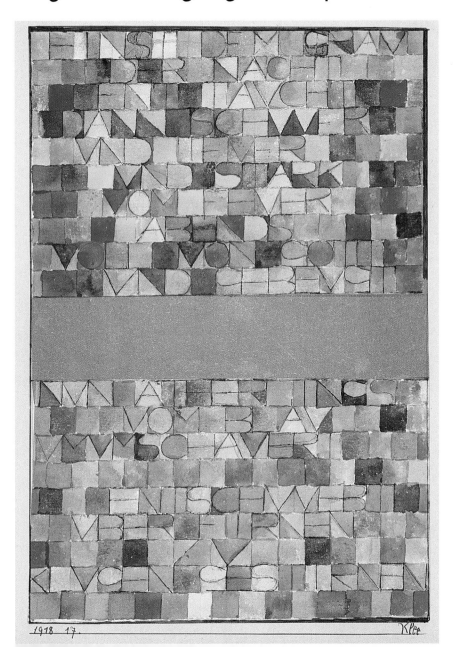

Time as a teacher

In 1920 Paul became a teacher at the Bauhaus.
This was the most famous art school in Germany.
Paul taught there until 1931.

24

Paul's pictures show what he taught at the
Bauhaus. He taught students that an artist is like
a tree trunk. The branches are the thoughts he
shows in his pictures.

Escape from Germany

A new **government,** called the **Nazis,** took power in Germany. They did not like Paul's pictures or those of many other artists. Paul had to move to Switzerland in 1933.

The Nazis wanted pictures to look like real things. Paul did not agree. He used his colours and lines to make people think for themselves.

Illness and death

Paul caught a disease when he was 56 years old. He never got better. He still painted but he was in constant pain. Paul died aged 61 on 29 June 1940.

Paul's illness made him think about death and war. His pictures became darker. Thick black lines replaced the bright colours he used when he was well.

Timeline

1879	Paul Klee born near Berne, Switzerland on 18 December.
1886	Paul begins to **study** the violin.
1889	Paul joins Berne Municipal **Orchestra**.
1893	Lumière brothers develop cinema in France.
1898	Paul leaves school and moves to Munich, Germany.
	The sculptor Henry Moore is born.
1903	The Wright brothers fly the first aeroplane.
1906	Paul marries Lily Stumpf and has **etchings exhibited**.
	The artist Paul Cézanne dies.
1910	Paul has successful exhibitions in Switzerland.
1911	Paul joins Der Blaue Reiter group of **expressionist** artists.
1913	Charlie Chaplin makes his first film.
1914	Paul visits Tunisia and decides to fill his pictures with colour.
1914-18	The First World War.
1920-31	Paul teaches at the famous Bauhaus art school in Germany.
1926	The artists Claude Monet and Mary Cassatt die.
1927	Charles Lindbergh makes first solo flight across the Atlantic.
1933	Paul forced to leave Germany and go to Switzerland.
1935	Paul begins a long illness.
1939	The Second World War begins in Europe.
1940	Paul dies in Muralto, Switzerland on 29 June.

Glossary

concert playing music in public

etching picture made by drawing on a metal plate and then printing it

exhibit to show and sell works of art in public

expressionist a type of art that changes the way things look to show feelings

government group of people who rule a country

graphic artist someone who makes pictures to print

language way of passing on ideas to other people

mosaics pattern of coloured stone used to make a picture

Nazi short name for the National Socialist German Workers' Party

orchestra group of musicians who play concerts in public

practise keep trying to do something to get better at it

study learn about a subject

More books to read

Looking at paintings: Cats, Peggy Roalf, Belitha Press

More paintings to see

Comedy, Paul Klee, Tate Gallery, London

Seaside Resort in the South of France, Paul Klee, Tate Gallery, London

Index